Going to School

BookLife

By
Grace
Jones

©2017
Book Life
King's Lynn
Norfolk PE30 4LS

ISBN: 978-1-78637-038-9

Written by:
Grace Jones

Designed by:
Ian McMullen

A catalogue record for this book
is available from the British Library.

Contents

Going to School

Child

All over the world children wake up early to go to school.

Walking

Bus

Bicycle

Children get to school by walking, cycling or by getting a bus.

5

What do we do at School?

Book

Pencil

At school, we learn how to read and write.

We get to play with our friends too.

Friends

Our Teacher

Map

Teacher

Our teacher helps us to learn.

If we have a problem, we can ask them for help by putting our hands up.

Hand

Arm

In Our Classroom

Book

Pencil

We learn and do our work in a classroom.

Blackboard

Teacher

Desk

Chair

There are lots of different things in our classroom to help us to learn.

What do we Learn?

We get taught maths and science.

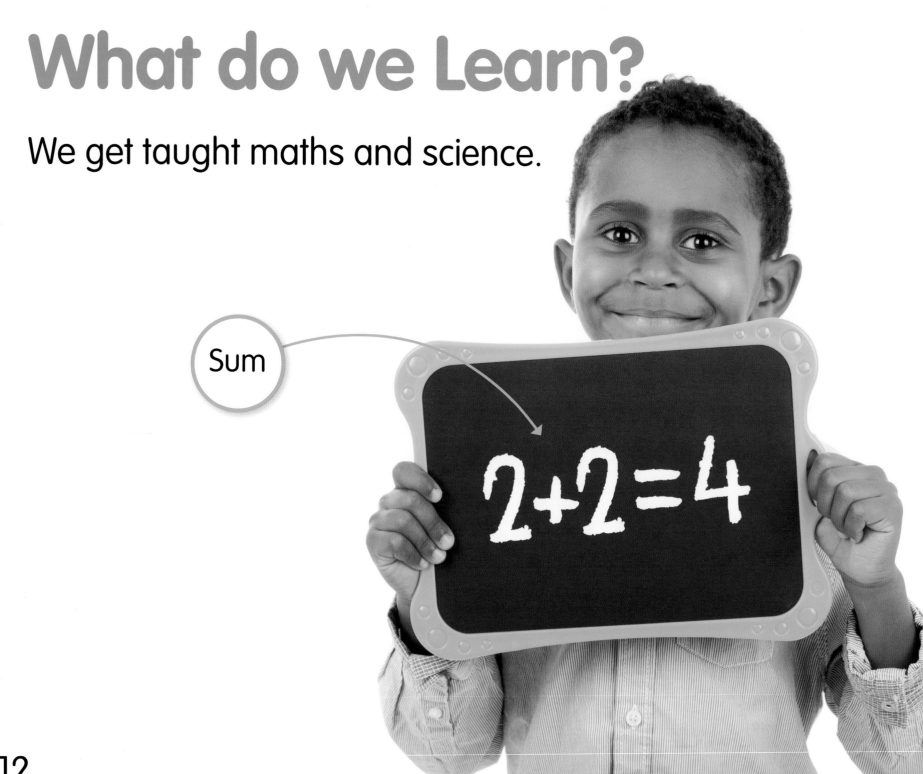

Sum

2+2=4

We have fun doing art and making music too.

Recorder

Guitar

Violin

Drum

What do we Wear?

At school we all wear the same clothes.

Shirt

Trousers

Skirt

Shoes

This is called a school uniform.

Bag

Jumper

Dress

Where do we Eat?

Fork

Plate

Drink

We eat our lunch in the school canteen.

A school cook gives us our food.

Kitchen

Cook

Food

17

Friends and Playtime

We see our friends at school.

We can play with our friends at break-time.

Skipping Rope

Football

Homework

Pen

Drink

Book

The teacher will give us work to do at home.

This is called homework.

Rules at School

Put your hand up if you need to ask a question.

Rules tell us how we should behave at school.

Be quiet when your teacher is speaking.

Index

Photo Credits

Abbreviations: l-left, r-right, b-bottom, t-top, c-centre, m-middle.

Front Cover l - MNStudio. Front Cover ml - wavebreakmedia. Front Cover mr - Rob Hainer. Front Cover r - Ilya Andriyanov. 2 - Sergey Novikov. 3 - Ilya Andriyanov. 4 - s_oleg. 5l - VaLiza. 5m - Pressmaster. 5r - Rob Hainer. 6inset - Anna Omelchenko. 6 - Zholobov Vadim. 7 - Sergey Novikov. 8 - wavebreakmedia. 9 - lassedesignen. 10 - Pressmaster. 11 - wavebreakmedia. 12 - Samuel Borges Photography. 13 - SpeedKingz. 14 - Sergiy Bykhunenko. 15 - Paul Michael Hughes. 16 - Oksana Kuzmina. 17 - SpeedKingz. 18 - oliveromg. 19 - bikeriderlondon. 20 - oliveromg. 21 - anekoho. 22 - Sergey Novikov. 23 - bbevren.
Images are courtesy of Shutterstock.com. With thanks to Getty Images, Thinkstock Photo and iStockphoto.